Plant Based

Diet Recipe Book

Discover the Benefits of Eating Well with High-protein Plant-Based Diet Recipes, Energize Your Body and Lose Weight Fast

Lisa Rice

Table of Contents

Introduction

A plant-based diet is a diet based primarily on whole plant foods. It is identical to the regular diet we're used to already, except that it leaves out foods that are not exclusively from plants. Hence, a plant-based diet does away with all types of animal-sourced foods, hydrogenated oils, refined sugars, and processed foods. A whole food plant-based diet comprises not just fruits and vegetables; it also consists of unprocessed or barely-processed oils with healthy monounsaturated fats (like extra-virgin olive oil), whole grains, legumes (essentially lentils and beans), seeds and nuts, as well as herbs and spices.

What makes a plant-based meal (or any meal) fun is the manner with which you make them; the seasoning process; and the combination process that contributes to a fantastic flavor and makes every meal unique and enjoyable. There are lots of delicious recipes (all plant-centered), which will prove helpful in when you intend making mouthwatering, healthy plant-based dishes for personal or household consumption. Provided you're eating these plant-based foods regularly, you'll have very problems with fat or diseases that result from bad dietary habits, and there would be no need for excessive calorie tracking.

Plant-based diet recipes are versatile; they range from colorful Salads to Lentil Stews, and Bean Burritos. The recipes also draw influences from around the globe, with Mexican, Chinese, European, Indian cuisines all part of the vast array of plant-based recipes available to choose from. Why You Ought to Reduce Your Intake of Processed and Animal-Based Foods. You have likely heard over and over that processed food has adverse effects on your health. You might have also been told repeatedly to stay away from foods with lots of preservatives; nevertheless, nobody ever offered any genuine or concrete facts about why you ought to avoid these foods and why they are unsafe. Consequently, let us properly dissect it to help you properly comprehend why you ought to stay away from these healthy eating offenders. They have massive habit-forming characteristics. Humans have a predisposition towards being addicted to some specific foods; however, the reality is that the fault is not wholly ours. Every one of the unhealthy treats we relish now and then triggers the dopamine release in our brains. This creates a pleasurable effect in our brain, but the excitement is usually short-lived. The discharged dopamine additionally causes an attachment connection gradually, and this is the reason some people consistently go back to eat certain unhealthy foods even when they know it's unhealthy and unnecessary. You can get rid of this by taking out that inducement completely. They are sugar-laden and plenteous in glucose-fructose syrup. Animal-based and processed foods are laden with refined sugars and glucose-fructose syrup which has almost no beneficial food nutrient. An ever-increasing number of studies are affirming what several people presumed from the start; that genetically modified foods bring about inflammatory bowel disease, which consequently makes it increasingly difficult for the body to assimilate essential nutrients. The disadvantages that result from your body being unable to assimilate essential nutrients from consumed foods rightly cannot be overemphasized. Processed and animal-based food products contain plenteous amounts of refined carbohydrates. Indeed, your body requires carbohydrates to give it the needed energy to run body capacities. In any case, refining carbs dispenses with the fundamental supplements; in the way that refining entire grains disposes of the whole grain part. What remains, in the wake of refining, is what's considered as empty carbs or empty calories. These can negatively affect the metabolic system in your body by sharply increasing your blood sugar and insulin quantities. They contain lots of synthetic

—

ingredients. At the point when your body is taking in non-natural ingredients, it regards them as foreign substances. Your body treats them as a health threat. Your body isn't accustomed to identifying synthetic compounds like sucralose or these synthesized sugars. Hence, in defense of your health against this foreign "aggressor," your body does what it's capable of to safeguard your health. It sets off an immune reaction to tackle this "enemy" compound, which indirectly weakens your body's general disease alertness, making you susceptible to illnesses. The concentration and energy expended by your body in ensuring your immune system remain safe could instead be devoted somewhere else. They contain constituent elements that set off an excitable reward sensation in your body. A part of processed and animal-based foods contain compounds like glucose-fructose syrup, monosodium glutamate, and specific food dyes that can trigger some addiction. They rouse your body to receive a benefit in return whenever you consume them. Monosodium glutamate, for example, is added to many store-bought baked foods. This additive slowly conditions your palates to relish the taste. It gets mental just by how your brain interrelates with your taste sensors.

This reward-centric arrangement makes you crave it increasingly, which ends up exposing you to the danger of over consuming calories.

For animal protein, usually, the expression "subpar" is used to allude to plant proteins since they generally have lower levels of essential amino acids as against animal-sourced protein. Nevertheless, what the vast majority don't know is that large amounts of essential amino acids can prove detrimental to your health. Let me break it down further for you.

5Amish Oats

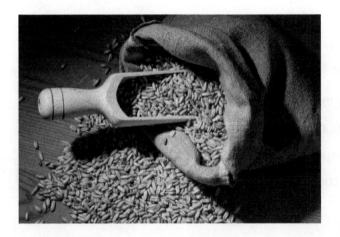

Preparation Time: 5 minutes

Cooking Time: 10 minutes

Servings: 4

Ingredients:

- 3 cups unsweetened almond milk or other non-dairy milk
- 2 1/2 cups old-fashioned rolled oats
- 2/3 cup sweetened dried cranberries
- 1/2 cup packed light brown sugar or maple syrup
- 1/2 cup toasted slivered blanched almonds or chopped walnuts
- 2 tablespoons vegan butter, melted
- 2 teaspoons pure vanilla extract
- 1 1/2 teaspoons ground cinnamon

1 1/2 teaspoons baking powder

1/2 teaspoon salt

Directions:

Lightly oil your Instant Pot insert with cooking spray.

In a bowl mix the almond milk, butter, vanilla, sugar, baking powder, salt, and cinnamon.

Stir in the oats, cranberries, and nuts.

Seal and cook on Beans for 12 minutes.

Nutrition:

Calories: 328

Fat: 13g

Protein: 38g

Carbohydrates: 8g

Sweet Pumpkin Quinoa.

Preparation Time: 5 minutes

Cooking Time: 40 minutes

Servings: 2

Ingredients:

4 cups unsweetened almond milk

1 cup quinoa, rinsed and drained

1/2 cup canned solid-pack pumpkin

1/4 cup pure maple syrup

1 teaspoon pure vanilla extract

1 teaspoon ground cinnamon

1/2 teaspoon salt

1/4 teaspoon ground ginger

1/4 teaspoon ground allspice

1/4 teaspoon ground nutmeg

Directions:

Spray the insert of your Instant Pot with cooking oil.

Add the **Ingredients:**.

Seal and cook on Stew for 38 minutes.

Depressurize naturally and serve.

Nutrition:

Calories: 299

Fat: 3g

Protein: 64g

Carbohydrates: 2g

Sauces, Dressings, and Dips

Satay Sauce

Preparation Time: 5 minutes

Cooking Time: 8 minutes

Servings: 2

Ingredients:

- ½ yellow onion, diced

- 3 garlic cloves, minced
- 1 fresh red chile, thinly sliced (optional)
- 1-inch (2.5-cm) piece fresh ginger, peeled and minced
- ¼ cup smooth peanut butter
- 2 tablespoons coconut aminos
- 1 (13.5-ounce / 383-g) can unsweetened coconut milk
- ¼ teaspoon freshly ground black pepper
- ¼ teaspoon salt (optional)

Directions:

1. Heat a large nonstick skillet over medium-high heat until hot.
2. Add the onion, garlic cloves, chile (if desired), and ginger to the skillet, and sauté for 2 minutes.
3. Pour in the peanut butter and coconut aminos and stir well. Add the coconut milk, black pepper, and salt (if desired) and continue whisking, or until the sauce is just beginning to bubble and thicken.
4. Remove the sauce from the heat to a bowl. Taste and adjust the seasoning if necessary.

Nutrition:

Calories: 322

Fat: 28.8g

Carbs: 9.4g

Protein: 6.3g

Fiber: 1.8g

Tahini BBQ Sauce

Preparation Time: 10 minutes

Cooking Time: 0 minutes

Servings: 4

ingredients:

- ½ cup water
- ¼ cup red miso
- 3 cloves garlic, minced
- 1-inch (2.5 cm) piece ginger, peeled and minced
- 2 tablespoons rice vinegar

- 2 tablespoons tahini
- 2 tablespoons chili paste or chili sauce
- 1 tablespoon date sugar
- ½ teaspoon crushed red pepper (optional)

Directions:

1. Place all the ingredients in a food processor, and purée until thoroughly mixed and smooth. You can thin the sauce out by stirring in ½ cup of water, or keep it thick.
2. Transfer to the refrigerator to chill until ready to serve.

Nutrition:

Calories: 206

Fat: 10.2g

Carbs: 21.3g

Protein: 7.2g

Fiber: 4.4g

Tamari Vinegar Sauce

Preparation Time: 10 minutes

Cooking Time: 0 minutes

Servings: 1

 Ingredients:

¼ cup tamari

½ cup nutritional yeast

2 tablespoons balsamic vinegar

2 tablespoons apple cider vinegar

2 tablespoons Worcestershire sauce

2 teaspoons Dijon mustard

1 tablespoon plus 1 teaspoon maple syrup

½ teaspoon ground turmeric

¼ teaspoon black pepper

Directions:

Place all the ingredients in an airtight container, and whisk until everything is well incorporated. Store in the refrigerator for up to 3 weeks.

Nutrition:

Calories: 216

Fat: 9.9g

Carbs: 18.0g

Protein: 13.7g

Fiber: 7.7g

Sweet and Tangy Ketchup

Preparation Time: 5 minutes

Cooking Time: 15 minutes

Servings: 2

Ingredients:

1 cup water

¼ cup maple syrup

1 cup tomato paste

3 tablespoons apple cider vinegar

1 teaspoon onion powder

1 teaspoon garlic powder

Directions:

Add the water to a medium saucepan and bring to a rolling boil over high heat.

Reduce the heat to low, stir in the maple syrup, tomato paste, vinegar, onion powder, and garlic powder. Cover and bring to a gently simmer for about 10 minutes, stirring frequently, or until the sauce begins to thicken and bubble.

Let the sauce rest for 30 minutes until cooled completely. Transfer to an airtight container and refrigerate for up to 1 month.

Nutrition:

Calories: 46

Fat: 5.2g

Carbs: 1.0g

Protein: 1.1g

Fiber: 1.0g

Homemade Tzatziki Sauce

Preparation Time: 20 minutes

Cooking Time: 0 minutes

Servings: 1

Ingredients:

2 ounces (57 g) raw, unsalted cashews (about ½ cup)

2 tablespoons lemon juice

1/3 cup water

1 small clove garlic

1 cup chopped cucumber, peeled

2 tablespoons fresh dill

Directions:

In a blender, add the cashews, lemon juice, water, and garlic. Keep it aside for at least 15 minutes to soften the cashews.

Blend the ingredients until smooth. Stir in the chopped cucumber and dill, and continue to blend until it reaches your desired consistency. It doesn't need to be totally smooth. Feel free to add more water if you like a thinner consistency.

Transfer to an airtight container and chill for at least 30 minutes for best flavors.

Bring the sauce to room temperature and shake well before serving.

Nutrition:

Calories: 208

Fat: 13.5g

Carbs:15.0 g

Protein: 6.7g

Fiber: 2.8g

Tangy Cashew Mustard Dressing

Preparation Time: 20 minutes

Cooking Time: 0 minutes

Servings: 1

Ingredients:

2 ounces (57 g) raw, unsalted cashews (about ½ cup)

½ cup water

3 tablespoons lemon juice

2 teaspoons apple cider vinegar

2 tablespoons Dijon mustard

1 medium clove garlic

Directions:

Put all the ingredients in a food processor and keep it aside for at least 15 minutes.

Purée until the ingredients are combined to a smooth and creamy mixture. Thin the dressing with a little extra water as needed to achieve your preferred consistency.

Store in an airtight container in the refrigerator for up to 5 days.

Nutrition:

Calories: 187

Fat: 13.0g

Carbs: 11.5g

Protein: 5.9g

Fiber: 1.7g

Avocado-dill Dressing

Preparation Time: 20 minutes

Cooking Time: 0 minutes

Servings: 1

Ingredients:

  2 ounces (57 g) raw, unsalted cashews (about ½ cup)

  ½ cup water

  3 tablespoons lemon juice

½ medium, ripe avocado, chopped

1 medium clove garlic

2 tablespoons chopped fresh dill

2 green onions, white and green parts, chopped

Directions:

Put the cashews, water, lemon juice, avocado, and garlic into a blender. Keep it aside for at least 15 minutes to soften the cashews.

Blend until everything is fully mixed. Fold in the dill and green onions, and blend briefly to retain some texture.

Store in an airtight container in the fridge for up to 3 days and stir well before serving.

Nutrition:

Calories: 312

Fat: 21.1g

Carbs: 22.6g

Protein: 8.0g

Fiber: 7.1g

Easy Lemon Tahini Dressing

Preparation Time: 5 minutes

Cooking Time: 0 minutes

Servings: 1

Ingredients:

½ cup tahini

¼ cup fresh lemon juice (about 2 lemons)

1 teaspoon maple syrup

1 small garlic clove, chopped

1/8 teaspoon black pepper

¼ teaspoon salt (optional)

¼ to ½ cup water

Directions:

Process the tahini, lemon juice, maple syrup, garlic, black pepper, and salt (if desired) in a blender (high-speed blenders work best for this). Gradually add the water until the mixture is completely smooth.

Store in an airtight container in the fridge for up to 5 days.

Nutrition:

Calories: 128

Fat: 9.6g

Carbs: 6.8g

Protein: 3.6g

Fiber: 1.9g

Sweet Mango and Orange Dressing

Preparation Time: 5 minutes

Cooking Time: 0 minutes

Servings: 1

Ingredients:

  1 cup (165 g) diced mango, thawed if frozen

  ½ cup orange juice

  2 tablespoons rice vinegar

  2 tablespoons fresh lime juice

  ¼ teaspoon salt (optional)

  1 teaspoon date sugar (optional)

2 tablespoons chopped cilantro

Directions:

Pulse all the ingredients except for the cilantro in a food processor until it reaches the consistency you like. Add the cilantro and whisk well.

Store in an airtight container in the fridge for up to 2 days.

Nutrition:

Calories: 32

Fat: 0.1g

Carbs: 7.4g

Protein: 0.3g

Fiber: 0.5g

Creamy Avocado Cilantro Lime Dressing

Preparation Time: 5 minutes

Cooking Time: 0 minutes

Servings: 2

Ingredients:

- 1 avocado, diced
- ½ cup water

- ¼ cup cilantro leaves
- ¼ cup fresh lime or lemon juice (about 2 limes or lemons)
- ½ teaspoon ground cumin
- ¼ teaspoon salt (optional)

Directions:

1. Put all the ingredients in a blender (high-speed blenders work best for this), and pulse until well combined. Taste and adjust the seasoning as needed. It is best served within 1 day.

Nutrition:

Calories: 94

Fat: 7.4g

Carbs: 5.7g

Protein: 1.1g

Fiber: 3.5g

Maple Dijon Dressing

Preparation Time: 5 minutes

Cooking Time: 0 minutes

Servings: 1

Ingredients:

- ¼ cup apple cider vinegar
- 2 teaspoons Dijon mustard
- 2 tablespoons maple syrup
- 2 tablespoons low-sodium vegetable broth
- ¼ teaspoon black pepper
- Salt, to taste (optional)

Directions:

2. Mix together the apple cider vinegar, Dijon mustard, maple syrup, vegetable broth, and black pepper in a resealable container until well incorporated. Season with salt to taste, if desired.

3. The dressing can be refrigerated for up to 5 days.

Nutrition:

Calories: 82

Fat: 0.3g

Carbs: 19.3g

Protein: 0.6g

Fiber: 0.7g

Avocado-chickpea Dip

Preparation Time: 15 minutes

Cooking Time: 0 minutes

Servings: 2

Ingredients:

- 1 (15-ounce / 425-g) can cooked chickpeas, drained and rinsed
- 2 large, ripe avocados, chopped
- ¼ cup red onion, finely chopped
- 1 tablespoon Dijon mustard
- 1 to 2 tablespoons lemon juice
- 2 teaspoons chopped fresh oregano
- 1/2 teaspoon garlic clove, finely chopped

Directions:

In a medium bowl, mash the cooked chickpeas with a potato masher or the back of a fork, or until the chickpeas pop open (a food processor works best for this).

Stir in the remaining ingredients and continue to mash until completely smooth.

Place in the refrigerator to chill until ready to serve.

Nutrition:

Calories: 101

Fat: 1.9g

Carbs: 16.2g

Protein: 4.7g

Fiber: 4.6g

Beer "Cheese" Dip

Preparation Time: 10 minutes

Cooking Time: 7 minutes

Servings: 3

Ingredients:

¾ cup water

¾ cup brown ale

½ cup raw walnuts, soaked in hot water for at least 15
minutes, then drained

½ cup raw cashews, soaked in hot water for at least 15
minutes, then drained

2 tablespoons tomato paste

2 tablespoons fresh lemon juice

1 tablespoon apple cider vinegar

½ cup nutritional yeast

½ teaspoon sweet or smoked paprika

1 tablespoon arrowroot powder

1 tablespoon red miso

Directions:

Place the water, brown ale, walnuts, cashews, tomato paste, lemon juice, and apple cider vinegar into a high-speed blender, and purée until thoroughly mixed and smooth.

Transfer the mixture to a saucepan over medium heat. Add the nutritional yeast, paprika, and arrowroot powder, and whisk well. Bring to a simmer for about 7 minutes, stirring frequently, or until the mixture begins to thicken and bubble.

Remove from the heat and whisk in the red miso. Let the dip cool for 10 minutes and refrigerate in an airtight container for up to 5 days.

Nutrition:

Calories: 113

Fat: 5.1g

Carbs: 10.4g

Protein: 6.3g

Fiber: 3.8g

Creamy Black Bean Dip

Preparation Time: 10 minutes

Cooking Time: 0 minutes

Servings: 3

Ingredients:

  4 cups cooked black beans, rinsed and drained

  2 tablespoons Italian seasoning

  2 tablespoons minced garlic

  2 tablespoon low-sodium vegetable broth

2 tablespoons onion powder

1 tablespoon lemon juice, or more to taste

¼ teaspoon salt (optional)

Directions:

In a large bowl, mash the black beans with a potato masher or the back of a fork until mostly smooth.

Add the remaining ingredients to the bowl and whisk to combine.

Taste and add more lemon juice or salt, if needed.

Serve immediately, or refrigerate for at least 30 minutes to better incorporate the flavors.

Nutrition:

Calories: 387

Fat: 6.5g

Carbs: 63.0g

Protein: 21.2g

Fiber: 16.0g

Spicy and Tangy Black Bean Salsa

Preparation Time: 15 minutes

Cooking Time: 0 minutes

Servings: 3

Ingredients:

- 1 (15-ounce / 425-g) can cooked black beans, drained and rinsed
- 1 cup chopped tomatoes
- 1 cup corn kernels, thaw if frozen
- ½ cup cilantro or parsley, chopped
- ¼ cup finely chopped red onion

1 tablespoon lemon juice

1 tablespoon lime juice

1 teaspoon chili powder

½ teaspoon ground cumin

½ teaspoon regular or smoked paprika

1 medium clove garlic, finely chopped

Directions:

Put all the ingredients in a large bowl and stir with a fork until well incorporated.

Serve immediately, or chill for 2 hours in the refrigerator to let the flavors blend.

Nutrition:

Calories: 83

Fat: 0.5g

Carbs: 15.4g

Protein: 4.3g

Fiber: 4.6g

Homemade Chimichurri

Preparation Time: 5 minutes

Cooking Time: 0 minutes

Servings: 1

Ingredients:

  1 cup finely chopped flat-leaf parsley leaves

  Zest and juice of 2 lemons

  ¼ cup low-sodium vegetable broth

  4 garlic cloves

  1 teaspoon dried oregano

Directions:

Place all the ingredients into a food processor, and pulse until it reaches the consistency you like. Refrigerate the chimichurri in an airtight container for up to 5 days. It's best served within 1 day.

Nutrition:

Calories: 19

Fat: 0.2g

Carbs: 3.7g

Protein: 0.7g

Fiber: 0.7g

Cilantro Coconut Pesto

Preparation Time: 5 minutes

Cooking Time: 0 minutes

Servings: 2

Ingredients:

1 (13.5-ounce / 383-g) can unsweetened coconut milk

2 jalapeños, seeds and ribs removed

1 bunch cilantro, leaves only

1 tablespoon white miso

1-inch (2.5 cm) piece ginger, peeled and minced

Water, as needed

Directions:

Pulse all the ingredients in a blender until creamy and
smooth.

51

Thin with a little extra water as needed to reach your preferred consistency.

Store in an airtight container in the fridge for up to 2 days or in the freezer for up to 6 months.

Nutrition:

Calories: 141

Fat: 13.7g

Carbs: 2.8g

Protein: 1.6g

Fiber: 0.3g

Fresh Mango Salsa

Preparation Time: 10 minutes

Cooking Time: 0 minutes

Servings: 6

Ingredients:

  2 small mangoes, diced

  1 red bell pepper, finely diced

  ½ red onion, finely diced

  Juice of ½ lime, or more to taste

  2 tablespoon low-sodium vegetable broth

  Handful cilantro, chopped

Freshly ground black pepper, to taste

Salt, to taste (optional)

Directions:

Stir together all the ingredients in a large bowl until well incorporated.

Taste and add more lime juice or salt, if needed.

Store in an airtight container in the fridge for up to 5 days.

Nutrition:

Calories: 86

Fat: 1.9g

Carbs: 13.3g

Protein: 1.2g

Fiber: 0.9g

Pineapple Mint Salsa

Preparation Time: 10 minutes

Cooking Time: 0 minutes

Servings: 3

Ingredients:

   1 pound (454 g) fresh pineapple, finely diced and juices
      reserved

   1 bunch mint, leaves only, chopped

   1 minced jalapeño, (optional)

   1 white or red onion, finely diced

   Salt, to taste (optional)

Directions:

In a medium bowl, mix the pineapple with its juice, mint, jalapeño (if desired), and onion, and whisk well. Season with salt to taste, if desired.

Refrigerate in an airtight container for at least 2 hours to better incorporate the flavors.

Nutrition:

Calories: 58

Fat: 0.1g

Carbs: 13.7g

Protein: 0.5g

Fiber: 1.0g

Keto Salsa Verde

Preparation time: 10 minutes

Cooking time: 5 minutes

Servings: 5

Ingredients:

 4 tablespoon fresh cilantro, finely chopped

 1/4 cup fresh parsley, finely chopped

 2 garlic cloves, grated

 2 teaspoon lemon juice

 3/4 cup of olive oil

 2 tablespoon small capers

 1 teaspoon of salt

 1/2 teaspoon black pepper

Directions:

 Add all **Ingredients:** to a large mixing bowl. Can be mixed with by hand or with an immersion blender. Mix until desired consistency is achieved.

 Can be served over burgers, sandwiches, salads and more. Can be stored in the refrigerator for up to 5 days or for longer in the freezer.

Nutrition:

Total Fat: 25.3g

Cholesterol: 0mg

Sodium: 475mg, Protein: 0.2g

Chimichurri

Preparation time: 10 minutes

Cooking time: 5 minutes

Servings: 8

Ingredients:

1/2 yellow bell pepper, deseeded and finely chopped

1 green chili pepper, deseeded and finely chopped

Juice and zest of 1 lemon

1 cup olive oil

1/2 cup parsley, chopped

2 garlic cloves, grated

Salt and pepper to taste

Directions:

Add all **Ingredients:** to a large mixing bowl. Can be mixed with by hand or with an immersion blender. Mix until desired consistency is achieved.

Can be served over burgers, sandwiches, salads and more. Can be stored in the refrigerator for up to 5 days or for longer in the freezer.

Nutrition:

Total Fat: 25.3g, Sodium: 3mg, Fiber: 2g

Keto Vegan Raw Cashew Cheese Sauce

Preparation time: 5 minutes

Cooking time: 5 minutes

Servings: 6

Ingredients:

- 1 cup raw cashews, soaked in water for at least 3 hours prior to making recipe
- 2 tablespoon olive oil
- 2 tablespoon nutritional yeast
- 1/4 teaspoon garlic powder
- 2 tablespoon fresh lemon juice
- 1/2 cup water
- Salt to taste

Directions:

To prepare cashews prior to making the sauce, boil 2 cups of water turn off heat and add cashews. This can be allowed to soak overnight. Rinse and strained cashews. Discard water.

Add all **Ingredients:** to a food processor and blend until a smooth consistency is achieved. Can be used to make pizzas, over roasted veggies, in lasagna, as a dip and more.

Nutrition:

Total Fat: 15.5g

Sodium: 34mg

Total carbohydrates: 9.23g

Protein: 5.1g

Spicy Avocado Mayonnaise

Preparation time: 10 minutes

Cooking time: 10 minutes

Servings: 8

Ingredients:

2 ripe avocados, pitted and peeled

1/4 jalapeno pepper, minced

2 tablespoon lemon juice

1/2 teaspoon onion powder

2 tablespoon fresh cilantro, chopped

Salt to taste

Directions:

Add all **Ingredients:** to a food processor and blender until a smooth creamy consistency is achieved.

The jalapeno peppers can be foregone if you prefer a cooler mayo. Can be enjoyed in sandwiches, on toast, as a topping, in veggie wraps and in salads

Nutrition:

Total Fat: 9.8g

Cholesterol: 0mg

Sodium: 23mg

Total carbohydrates: 4.6g

Dietary Fiber: 3.4g, Protein: 1g

Cauliflower Rice Wok

Preparation Time: 10 minutes

Cooking Time: 20 minutes

Serving: 4

Ingredients

- 1 lb. (450 g) tofu
- 1/2 cup (150 g) peas
- 1 tablespoon ginger
- 3 garlic cloves, minced
- 1/4 cup (30 g) green onions
- 1 cauliflower head, riced
- 2 carrots, diced
- 2 tablespoons sesame oil
- 3 tablespoons cashews
- 3 tablespoons soy sauce

Direction

1. Press and drain the tofu. Then crumble it slightly in a bowl. Set aside.

2. Add oil to a wok pan and place over medium heat. Cook garlic and ginger. Add the tofu and

stir for about 6 minutes, until golden and well cooked. Set the tofu aside.

3. Fill more oil to the pan and cook the carrots.
4. Mix peas along with the cauliflower rice. Cook for 7 minutes. Add the green onions, cooked tofu, cashews and soy sauce.
5. Serve the cauliflower fried rice and garnish with the sesame seeds. Enjoy!

Nutrition:

47 Calories

2.14g Protein

3.2g Fiber

Keto Strawberry Jam

Preparation time: 25 minutes

Cooking time: 5 minutes

Servings: 18

Ingredients:

   1 cup fresh strawberries, chopped

   1 tablespoon lemon juice

   4 teaspoon xylitol

   1 tablespoon water

Directions:

Add all **Ingredients:** to a small saucepan and place over medium heat. Stir to combine and cook for about 15 minutes. Stir occasionally.

After 15 minutes are up, mash-up strawberries with a potato masher or fork.

Pour into a heat-safe container such as a mason jar.

Allow to cool then cover with a lid and refrigerate. Can be stored in the refrigerator for up to 3 days. Goes great with toast and sweet sandwiches.

Nutrition:

Total Fat: 0g

Cholesterol: 0mg

Sodium: 0mg

Total carbohydrates: 1g

Dietary Fiber: 0.2g

Protein: 0.1g

Boulders Bean Burgers

Preparation Time: 10 minutes

Cooking Time: 10 minutes

Serving: 4

Ingredients

- 1 tablespoon olive oil
- ¼ cup couscous
- ¼ cup boiling water
- 1 (15-ounce) can white beans
- 2 tablespoons balsamic vinegar
- 2 tablespoons chopped sun-dried tomatoes or olives
- ½ teaspoon garlic powder
- ½ teaspoon salt
- 4 burger buns

Direction

1. Preheat the oven to 350°F.
2. Grease rimmed baking sheet with olive oil or line it with parchment paper. Mix couscous and boiling water.

3. Cover and set aside for about 5 minutes. Once the couscous is soft and the water is absorbed, fluff it with a fork. Add the beans, and mash them to a chunky texture. Add the vinegar, olive oil, sun-dried tomatoes, garlic powder, and salt; stir until combined but still a bit chunky.

4. Portion mixture into 4, and shape each into a patty. Put the patties on the prepared baking sheet, and bake for 25 to 30 minutes. Alternatively, heat some olive oil in a large skillet over medium heat, then add the patties, making sure each has oil under it.

5. Fry for about 5 minutes. Flip, adding more oil as needed, and fry for about 5 minutes more. Serve.

Nutrition:

315 Calories

12g Fiber

16g Protein

Keto Caramel Sauce

Preparation time: 10 minutes

Cooking time: 35 minutes

Servings: 8

Ingredients:

1/2 cup raw cashews

1/2 cup coconut cream, melted

10 drops liquid stevia

2 tablespoon vegan butter

3 teaspoon vanilla extract

A pinch of salt

Directions:

Preheat your oven to 325 degrees F

Place nuts on a greased baking tray and toast for 20 minutes or until lightly golden and crunchy.

Allow the nuts to cool slightly then add to a food processor and blend to a slightly lumpy consistency.

Add remaining **Ingredients:** and blend until a smooth and creamy consistency is achieved. Do not over blend or the coconut cream will become separated from the rest of the **Ingredients:**.

Can be stored in a glass, airtight container in the
refrigerator if not being served immediately. To
reheat the caramel to make it more flow able, add
to a saucepan and gently warm on low heat. Can be
served with your favorite keto vegan treats such as
ice-cream.

Nutrition:

Total Fat: 9.8g

Cholesterol: 0mg

Sodium: 29mg

Total carbohydrates: 4.6g

Instant Peas Risotto

Preparation Time: 10 min.

Cooking Time: 10 min.

Servings: *3*

Ingredients:

- 1 cup baby green peas
- 1 cup Arborio rice
- 2 cloves garlic, diced
- 3 tablespoons olive oil
- 1 brown onion, diced
- ½ teaspoon salt
- 2 celery sticks, make small cubes
- ½ teaspoon pepper
- 2 tablespoons lemon juice
- 2 cups vegetable stock

Directions:

1. Take your Instant Pot and place it on a clean kitchen platform. Turn it on after plugging it into a power socket.
2. Put the pot on "Saute" mode. In the pot, add the oil, celery, onions, pepper, and salt; cook

for 4-5 minutes until the ingredients become soft.

3. Mix in the zest, stock, garlic, peas, and rice. Stir the ingredients.

4. Close the lid and lock. Ensure that you have sealed the valve to avoid leakage.

5. Press "Manual" mode and set timer for 5 minutes. It will take a few minutes for the pot to build inside pressure and start cooking.

6. After the timer reads zero, press "Cancel" and quick release pressure.

7. Carefully remove the lid, add the lemon juice and serve warm!

Nutrition:

Calories - 362

Fat – 13g

Carbohydrates – 52.5g

Fiber – 3g

Protein – 8g

Keto Vegan Ranch Dressing

Preparation time: 5 minutes

Cooking time: 10 minutes

Servings: 3

Ingredients:

1 cup vegan mayo

1 1/2 cup coconut milk

2 scallions

2 garlic cloves, peeled

1 cup fresh dill

1 teaspoon garlic powder

Salt and pepper to taste

Directions:

Add scallion, fresh dill and garlic cloves to a food processor and pulse until finely chopped.

Add the rest of the **Ingredients:** and blend until a smooth, creamy consistency is achieved. Makes a great creamy salad dressing. Store in the refrigerator.

Nutrition:

Total Fat: 11.9g

Cholesterol: 0mg

Sodium: 50mg ,Fiber: 4g

Cauliflower Hummus

Preparation time: 10 minutes

Cooking time: 20 minutes

Servings: 7

Ingredients:

- 1 large head cauliflower
- 1 tablespoon almond butter
- 1 garlic clove, finely chopped
- 1 tablespoon lemon juice
- 2 teaspoon olive oil

1/4 teaspoon cumin

Salt and pepper to taste

Directions:

Cut cauliflower into florets and place in a large microwave-safe bowl. Microwave for 10 minutes on high heat or until completely cooked through.

Transfer cauliflower florets to a food processor. Add the rest of the **Ingredients:**.

Blend until smooth, creamy consistency is reached. Can be stored in the refrigerator in an airtight container for up to 5 days. Makes a great dip for fruits and veggies.

Nutrition:

Total Fat: 2.7g

Cholesterol: 0mg

Sodium: 12mg

Total carbohydrates: 2.7g

Catalina Dressing

Preparation time: 5 minutes

Cooking time: 0 minutes

Servings: 12

Ingredients:

- Dry mustard, one half teaspoon
- Chili powder, one half teaspoon
- Onion powder, one half teaspoon
- Apple cider vinegar, three tablespoons
- Olive oil, one quarter cup
- Tomato sauce, one quarter cup

Directions:

1. Mix well and store in the refrigerator.

Nutrition:

Calories: 47

Fat: 4.3

Fiber: 1.5

Carbs: 2.4

Protein: 2.4

Coleslaw Dressing

Preparation time: 5 minutes

Cooking time: 0 minutes

Servings: 12

Ingredients:

- Celery seed, one teaspoon
- Onion powder, one teaspoon
- Agave nectar, one tablespoon
- Dijon mustard, one tablespoon
- Apple cider vinegar, two tablespoons
- Vegenaise (vegan mayo), one half cup

Directions:

2. Mix well and store in the refrigerator.

Nutrition:

Calories: 47

Fat: 0.3

Fiber: 1.5

Carbs: 0.4

Protein: 0.4

Walnut Basil Dressing

Preparation time: 10 minutes

Cooking time: 0 minutes

Servings: 12

Ingredients:

Water, two to four tablespoons as needed

Salt, one quarter teaspoon

Garlic, minced, one tablespoon

Lemon juice, three tablespoons

Nutritional yeast, one quarter cup

Olive oil, one quarter cup

Walnuts, one-half cup crushed

Basil leaves, one cup packed loosely, chopped fine

Directions:

Mix all of the **Ingredients:** in a food processor or blender until smooth. Add spoons of water as needed to maintain a thick but workable consistency.

The finished product should resemble a pesto sauce.

Nutrition:

Calories: 89,Fat: 0.3, Fiber: 1.5, Carbs: 0.4 Protein: 0.4

Moroccan Carrot Dip

Preparation time: 15 minutes

Cooking time: 0 minutes

Servings: 1

Ingredients:

Water, one half cup

Black pepper, one quarter teaspoon

Salt, one half teaspoon

Fennel, one quarter teaspoon

Coriander, ground, one half teaspoon

Cumin, ground, one half teaspoon

Cinnamon, one teaspoon

Ginger, ground, one teaspoon

Garlic, minced, one tablespoon

Apple cider vinegar, two teaspoons

Cashews, raw, one third cup

Carrot, raw, one cup cut into small chunks

Directions:

Puree all of the listed **Ingredients:** until everything is smooth and creamy.

Nutrition:

Calories: 110

Fat: 0.3

Fiber: 1.5

Carbs: 0.4

Protein: 0.4

Tahini Citrus Dressing

Preparation time: 15 minutes

Cooking time: 0 minutes

Servings: 1 cup

Ingredients:

Black pepper, one half teaspoon

Salt, one half teaspoon

Garlic, minced, one tablespoon

Ginger, ground, one teaspoon

Dijon mustard, two teaspoons

Agave nectar, two tablespoons

Apple cider vinegar, one tablespoon

Tahini, two tablespoons

Lemon juice, one tablespoon

Orange juice, three tablespoons

Directions:

Mix all of the **Ingredients:** that are listed in a blender until they are creamy and smooth.

Nutrition:

Calories: 98

Fat: 0.3

Fiber: 1.5

Carbs: 0.4, Protein: 0.4

Curried Almond Dressing

Preparation time: 15 minutes

Cooking time: 8 minutes

Servings: 1 cup

Ingredients:

Curry powder, one eighth teaspoon

Black pepper, one eighth teaspoon

Salt, one half teaspoon

Dijon mustard, one half teaspoon

Ginger, ground, one teaspoon

Garlic, minced, one tablespoon

Water, two-thirds cup

Agave nectar, two tablespoons

Apple cider vinegar, two tablespoons

Almonds, raw, one half cup

Directions:

Puree well all of the **Ingredients:** in a blender until
they are creamy and smooth.

Nutrition:

Calories: 85

Fat: 0.3

Fiber: 1.5

Carbs: 0.4

Protein: 0.4

Applesauce Salad Dressing

Preparation time: 5 minutes

Cooking time: 8 minutes

Servings: 12

Ingredients:

Black pepper, one eighth teaspoon

Salt, one quarter teaspoon

Cinnamon, one teaspoon

Cumin, one quarter teaspoon

Dijon mustard, one teaspoon

Chickpea miso, one teaspoon

Balsamic vinegar, one tablespoon

Apple cider vinegar, two tablespoons

Applesauce, unsweetened, one quarter cup

Directions:

Mix well in a blender.

Nutrition:

Calories: 105

Fat: 0.3

Fiber: 1.5

Carbs: 0.4

Protein: 0.4

Balsamic Vinaigrette

Preparation time: 5 minutes

Cooking time: 8 minutes

Servings: 1 cup

Ingredients:

Black pepper, one quarter teaspoon

Salt, one quarter teaspoon

Garlic powder, one quarter teaspoon

Agave nectar, one tablespoon

Dijon mustard, one tablespoon

Balsamic vinegar, one quarter cup

Olive oil, one half cup

Directions:

Mix well in a blender or in a shaker jar.

Nutrition:

Calories: 91

Fat: 0.3

Fiber: 1.5

Carbs: 0.4

Protein: 0.4

Chipotle Lime Dressing

Preparation time: 5 minutes

Cooking time: 8 minutes

Servings: 1 cup

Ingredients:

Garlic powder, one quarter teaspoon

Paprika, one quarter teaspoon

Agave nectar, one tablespoon

Red pepper, one chopped

Lime juice, three tablespoons

Vegenaise, three tablespoons

Directions:

Mix well in a shaker jar or in a blender.

Nutrition:

Calories: 32

Fat: 0.3

Fiber: 1.5

Carbs: 0.4

Protein: 0.4

White Beans Dip

Preparation time: 15 minutes

Cooking time: 15 minutes

Servings: 6

Ingredients:

1/2 cup olive oil

2 tablespoons garlic cloves, chopped

2 (15.8-ounce) cans white beans, drained and rinsed

1/4 cup fresh lemon juice

4 tablespoons fresh parsley, chopped and divided

1 teaspoon ground cumin

1/4 tablespoon salt

1 teaspoon ground white pepper

Directions:

In a small saucepan, place the olive oil and garlic over medium-low heat and cook for about 2 minutes, stirring continuously.

Remove the pan of garlic oil from heat and let it cool slightly.

Strain the garlic oil, reserving both the oil and garlic in separate bowls.

In a food processor, place the beans, garlic, lemon juice, 2 tablespoons of parsley, and cumin, and pulse until smooth.

While motor is running, add the reserved oil and pulse until light and smooth.

Transfer the dip into a bowl and stir in salt and white pepper.

Serve with the garnishing of remaining parsley.

Nutrition:

Calories 263

Total Fat 18.1 g

Saturated Fat 2.5 g

Cholesterol 0 mg

Sodium 630 mg

Total Carbs 20.2 g

Fiber 5.7 g

Sugar 0.3 g

Protein 7 g

Edamame Hummus

Preparation time: 15 minutes

Cooking time: 11 minutes

Servings: 5

Ingredients:

10 ounces frozen edamame pods

1 ripe avocado, peeled, pitted, and chopped roughly

1/2 cup fresh cilantro, chopped

1/4 cup scallion, chopped

1 jalapeño pepper

1 garlic clove, peeled

2–3 tablespoons fresh lime juice

Salt and ground black pepper, to taste

1/4 cup avocado oil

2 tablespoons fresh basil leaves

Directions:

In a small pot of boiling water, cook the edamame
pods edamame pods for 6–8 minutes.

Drain the edamame pods and let them cool
completely.

Remove soybeans from the pods.

In a food processor, add edamame and remaining

Ingredients: (except for oil) and pulse until

mostly pureed.

While motor is running, add the reserved oil and pulse

until light and smooth.

Transfer the hummus into a bowl and serve with the

garnishing of remaining basil leaves.

Nutrition:

Calories 339

Total Fat 33.8 g

Saturated Fat 4.3 g

Cholesterol 0 mg

Sodium 27 mg

Total Carbs 6.3 g

Fiber 3.1 g

Sugar 0.3 g

Protein 5.1 g

Beans Mayonnaise

Preparation time: 10 minutes

Cooking time: 2 minutes

Servings: 4

Ingredients:

   1 (15-ounce) can white beans, drained and rinsed

   2 tablespoons apple cider vinegar

   1 tablespoon fresh lemon juice

   2 tablespoons yellow mustard

   3/4 teaspoon salt

   2 garlic cloves, peeled

   2 tablespoons aquafaba (liquid from the can of beans)

Directions:

In a food processor, add all **Ingredients:** (except for oil) and pulse until mostly pureed.

While motor is running, add the reserved oil and pulse until light and smooth.

Transfer the mayonnaise into a container and refrigerate to chill before serving.

Nutrition:

Calories 8

Total Fat 1.1 g

Saturated Fat 0.1 g

Cholesterol 0 mg

Sodium 559 mg

Total Carbs 14.3 g

Fiber 4.1 g

Sugar 0.2 g

Protein 5.2 g

Cashew Cream

Preparation time: 10 minutes

Cooking time: 0 minutes

Servings: 5

Ingredients:

- 1 cup raw, unsalted cashews, soaked for 12 hours and drained
- 1/2 cup water
- 1 tablespoon nutritional yeast
- 1 teaspoon fresh lemon juice

1/8 teaspoon salt

Directions:

In a food processor, add all **Ingredients:** and pulse on high speed until creamy and smooth.

Serve immediately.

Nutrition:

Calories 165

Total Fat 12.8 g

Saturated Fat 2.5 g

Cholesterol 0 mg

Sodium 65 mg

Total Carbs 9.9 g

Fiber 1.3 g

Sugar 1.4 g

Protein 5.1 g

Lemon Tahini

Preparation time: 15 minutes

Cooking time: 0 minutes

Servings: 4

Ingredients:

1/4 cup fresh lemon juice

4 medium garlic cloves, pressed

1/2 cup tahini

1/2 teaspoon fine sea salt

Pinch of ground cumin

6 tablespoons ice water

Directions:

In a medium bowl, combine the lemon juice and garlic and set aside for 10 minutes.

Through a fine-mesh sieve, strain the mixture into another medium bowl, pressing the garlic solids. Discard the garlic solids.

In the bowl of lemon juice, add the tahini, salt, and cumin, and whisk until well blended.

Slowly, add water, 2 tablespoons at a time, whisking well after each addition.

Nutrition:

Calories 187

Total Fat 16.3 g

Saturated Fat 2.4 g

Cholesterol 0 mg

Sodium 273 mg

Total Carbs 7.7 g

Fiber 2.9 g

Sugar 0.5 g

Protein 5.4 g

Keto-Vegan Ketchup

Preparation time: 35 minutes

Cooking time: 11 minutes

Servings: 12

Ingredients:

1/8 t of the following:

Mustard powder

Cloves, ground

1/4 t. paprika

1/2 t. garlic powder

3/4 t. onion powder

1 t. sea salt

3 tablespoon. apple cider vinegar

1/4 c. powdered monk fruit

1 c. water

6 oz. tomato paste

Directions:

In a little saucepan, whisk together all the

Ingredients:.

Cover the pan and bring to low heat and simmer for 30 minutes, stirring occasionally.

Once reduced, add to the blender and puree until it's a smooth consistency.

Nutrition:

Calories: 13

Carbohydrates: 2 g

Proteins: 0 g

Fats: 0 g

Avocado Hummus

Preparation time: 5 minutes

Cooking time: 5 minutes

Servings: 6

Ingredients:

1 tablespoon. cilantro, finely chopped

1/8 t. cumin

1 clove garlic

3 tablespoon. lime juice

1 1/2 tablespoon. of the following:

Tahini

Olive oil

2 avocados, medium cored & peeled

15 oz. chickpeas, drained

Salt and pepper to taste

Directions:

In a food processor, add garlic, lime juice, tahini, olive oil, and chickpeas and pulse until combined.

Add cumin and avocados and blend until smooth consistency approximately 2 minutes.

Add salt and pepper to taste.

Nutrition:

Calories: 310

Carbohydrates: 26 g

Proteins: 8 g

Fats: 20 g

Guacamole

Preparation time: 5 minutes

Cooking time: 5 minutes

Servings: 6

Ingredients:

3 tablespoon of the following:

Tomato, diced

Onion, diced

2 tablespoon of the following:

Cilantro, chopped

Jalapeno juice

1/4 t. garlic powder

1/2 t. salt

1/2 lime, squeezed

2 big avocados

1 jalapeno, diced

Directions:

Using a molcajete, crush the diced jalapenos until soft.

Add the avocados to the molcajete.

Squeeze the lime juice from ½ of the lime on top of the avocados.

Add the jalapeno juice, garlic, and salt and mix until smooth.

Once smooth, add in the onion, cilantro, and tomato and stir to incorporate.

Nutrition:

Calories: 127

Carbohydrates: 9.3 g

Proteins: 2.4 g

Fats: 10.2 g

Keto-Vegan Mayo

Preparation time: 5 minutes

Cooking time: 5 minutes

Servings: 6

Ingredients:

1/2 c. of the following:

Extra virgin olive oil

Almond milk, unsweetened

1/4 t. xanthan gum

Pinch of white pepper, ground

Pinch of Himalayan salt

1 t. Dijon mustard

2 t. apple cider vinegar

Directions:

In a blender, place milk, pepper salt, mustard, and vinegar.

Turn the blender to high speed and slowly add xanthan then the olive oil.

Remove from the blender and allow cooling for 2 hours in the refrigerator.

During cooling, the mixture will thicken.

Nutrition:

Calories: 160.4

Carbohydrates: 0.2 g

Proteins: 0 g

Fats: 18 g

Conclusion

In a nutshell, this cookbook offers you a world full of options to diversify your plant-based menu. People on this diet are usually seen struggling to choose between healthy food and flavor but, soon, they run out of the options. The selection of 250 recipes in this book is enough to adorn your dinner table with flavorsome, plant-based meals every day. Give each recipe a good read and try them out in the kitchen. You will experience tempting aromas and binding flavors every day.

The book is conceptualized with the idea of offering you a comprehensive view of a plant-based diet and how it can benefit the body. You may find the shift sudden, especially if you are a die-hard fan of non-vegetarian items. But you need not give up anything that you love. Eat everything in moderation.

The next step is to start experimenting with the different recipes in this book and see which ones are your favorites. Everyone has their favorite food, and you will surely find several of yours in this book. Start with breakfast and work your way through. You will be pleasantly surprised at how tasty a vegan meal really can be.

You will love reading this book, as it helps you to understand how revolutionary a plant-based diet can be. It will help you to make informed decisions as you move toward greater change for the greater good. What are you waiting for? Have you begun your journey on the path of the plant-based diet yet? If you haven't, do it now!

Now you have everything you need to get started making budget-friendly, healthy plant-based recipes. Just follow your basic shopping list and follow your meal plan to get started! It's easy to switch over to a plant-based diet if you have your meals planned out and temptation locked away. Don't forget to clean out your kitchen before starting, and you're sure to meet all your diet and health goals.

You need to plan if you are thinking about dieting. First, you can start slowly by just eating one meal a day, which is vegetarian and gradually increasing your number of vegetarian meals. Whenever you are struggling, ask your friend or family member to support you and keep you motivated. One important thing is also to be regularly accountable for not following the diet.

If dieting seems very important to you and you need to do it right, then it is recommended that you visit a professional such as a nutritionist or dietitian to discuss your dieting plan and optimizing it for the better.

No matter how much you want to lose weight, it is not advised that you decrease your calorie intake to an unhealthy level. Losing weight does not mean that you stop eating. It is done by carefully planning meals.

A plant-based diet is very easy once you get into it. At first, you will start to face a lot of difficulties, but if you start slowly, then you can face all the barriers and achieve your goal.

Swap out one unhealthy food item each week that you know is not helping you and put in its place one of the plant-based ingredients that you like. Then have some fun creating the many different recipes in this book. Find out what recipes you like the most so you can make them often and most of all; have some fun exploring all your recipe options.

Wish you good luck with the plant-based diet!

9 781801 833226